Taking the Headache Out of Finding Volunteers

Judy Wortley

David C. Cook Publishing Co.
Elgin, Illinois—Weston, Ontario

With deep gratitude
to my mentor
David B. Vasquez

THE RECRUITING REMEDY

By Judy Wortley

Published by DAVID C. COOK PUBLISHING CO.
850 N. Grove Ave., Elgin, IL 60120
Cable address: DCCOOK
Edited and designed by Dave and Neta Jackson
Cover design by Loran Berg
Cartoons by Rob Portlock
Illustrations by Dale Gehris
Printed in the United States of America
ISBN: 1-55513-331-2

CONTENTS

INTRODUCTION

Judy! My parents are going to be in town this weekend," Cathy told me on Friday morning (my day off, of course). "I forgot to tell you. I realize this is late notice, but I hope you'll be able to find a sub for my class this week." Akkkk!

This was the fourth telephone call of the week of a similar nature. Okay, who haven't I called this week that's already told me no? My sub list just isn't long enough to meet the need! (My sub list? What about the regular list? Is there any end to this?)

Oh, great! I just had my first volunteer in months call me and express a desire to teach Sunday school. I need someone (anyone!) in the two year old class, a real answer to prayer. But where does she want to teach? The fourth grade! Now what do I do? Tell her I don't need her? I desperately need her!—in the two year olds!

Now what? It's 9:50 P.M. Saturday night. James, teacher of the sixth grade, just telephoned with a case of the stomach flu. "I can't possibly make it to class tomorrow, I'm just too sick. Sorry!" Should I combine his class with another? Maybe I can still find someone willing to fill in for tomorrow.

Sound familiar? Recruitment and staffing are probably the most talked about subjects in the world of Christian education. The Sunday school is the world's largest volunteer organization. More men and women serve in the Sunday school than any other area of volunteer work in the entire world. Ninety percent of those volunteers work with children. But somehow more volunteers are always needed!

Recent years have seen a dramatic change in the secular world. The fast pace of American life leaves little time for volunteer activities. Many people give what little time is left over to Sunday mornings at the lake, sleeping in, or perhaps a child's soccer tournament. Working mothers have increased so rapidly—65 percent of preschool and elementary kids are now in homes with two incomes—three and a half times as many as in 1948. Divorce has created a multitude of single-parent families. These parents, mostly custodial mothers, are struggling to make ends meet and to keep emotions under control. "Such men and women—their numbers are increasing in our society—may expend so much energy coping with the daily stress of living that there is little time, strength or enthusiasm left over for parenting" (David Elkind, *The Hurried Child*).

Not only is there little energy left over for parenting, but there is little time, energy, or enthusiasm left over for volunteer work or ministry. The immense job of placing volunteers in service continues to loom before the church. The "me" generation has hung on. Do your own thing. Take care of yourself. If it's too hard, skip it. Financial pressures continue to drive the number of working mothers even higher. Recruit volunteers for children's ministry? Not an easy job in today's society! It will be even more difficult in the years ahead.

But there is hope. Imagine the excitement that will come when you have a list of people waiting for the coveted job of ministering to children! An impossible dream? A challenge—yes. Impossible—no.

The fact that you purchased this book shows you care about the children in your church—children that are in all stages and walks of life, some hurt, some without parents, some from churched homes, some from non-churched homes, some easy to love, others not so easy. In your heart and mind, look into the future and see that these children will become men and women who will impact our world, some with positive influence, some with negative influence. The influence of the church, through the individual volunteer, may alter the course of their lives. The smallest hug, smile, or act of kindness, done in the power and through the name of our Lord Jesus, could greatly affect major decisions made in their teen years and as young adults. As the church, we want to be a part of those decisions! The heart of your ministry is the precious volunteer—the hands and feet He uses to perpetuate His work.

This book is organized into two parts. Part 1 contains nine keys to successful recruitment. Part 2 presents five keys to effectively supporting your volunteers once they join the team. Please make this book your own—complete the activities, adapt the suggestions to fit your program, and let these ideas spark ideas of your own. With the Lord's help, your volunteers will come to see what a privilege it is to work with children. And may they come to see that those who work with children learn and laugh and grow as much as, if not more than, the children themselves.

While this book specifically addresses recruiting for children's ministry, the principles I talk about can be applied to recruiting any type of church worker. These principles will also work whether you have to recruit one or one hundred volunteers. These ideas have grown out of my experience in the church—both my successes and failures. I offer them to you as a co-laborer in the Lord's work. Thank you for your faithful service. May the Lord bless your recruiting efforts.

Part 1

RECRUITMENT

ESTABLISH

your philosophy of children's ministry

"If we start walking now, we can hit them all by the year 2525!"

When you have mastered this key, you will be able to:

- *Write out your philosophy of children's ministry.*
- *Share that philosophy with teachers and helpers.*
- *Explain your philosophy to your congregation.*

How to Establish A Philosophy of Children's Ministry

In order to be effective in your recruitment efforts, there are some basic principles that you must establish from the beginning. One of those is the formation of your philosophy of children's ministry.

Decide Where You Are Going

If you don't know clearly where you are going and what you want to accomplish, you will find it difficult to ask others to join forces with you in ministering to children. If no one leads, no one will follow.

Your philosophy must be the hallmark of your ministry! Every volunteer that works with you must be aware of it. You need to constantly put this philosophy before the congregation and the staff with which you work.

An effective philosophy can be easily stated in one sentence. This way those who work with you will not only be able to remember it, they will be able to share the philosophy with the parents in your congregation as well as others who may be looking for a church with a good program for children. You will also find that a clearly stated philosophy helps focus your total ministry.

My personal philosophy is simply stated: "Every child entering our church should feel loved and valued as an individual." There could be any number of philosophy statements that would describe your ministry. Some other suggestions might be:

- "To help every child know he or she has a special place in the household of God."
- "To lead each child into a personal relationship with Jesus Christ."
- "To help every child stand alone for Christ in the neighborhood and at school."

Once you have written out your philosophy, you will need to test it with the senior leadership of your church. The support of your pastor as well as other church staff will be essential if the philosophy is to succeed. See your pastor as a friend and partner in ministry.

Promote Your Philosophy

Once you have established a clear philosophy of children's ministry, it is important to communicate it so current teachers and helpers, future team members, and the whole church can work toward the same goals.

Here are some practical keys to propagating that philosophy:

Use it as a platform for all your basic announcements regarding children's ministry.

Develop a logo to go with your statement. Your logo can be simple or elabo-

Every child entering our church should feel loved and valued as an individual.

rate. If you are not artistic, you may want to ask a volunteer to create something for you, or you might simply adapt one of the enclosed samples. (See Resource I-1A.) Good clip art books are also available for your convenience in creating your logo.

If you have a regularly published church newsletter, use that vehicle to talk about the great things happening in children's ministry.

I've found it valuable to keep a record of special moments the Sunday school teachers tell me about. Sometimes it is a relationship that has arisen between the teacher and a child. Sometimes it is an incident that changed the life of a teacher or perhaps altered the course of a child's life. I write down these incidents to share later with my congregation. And when I do, I always include somewhere a reference to my philosophy of ministry.

During your teacher training meetings share with the teachers their importance to the individual child, including in that message your philosophy. Soon those who work with you will begin to clearly see they are part of something very significant and catch the vision you have for that ministry.

If you are just beginning in your ministry to children, it may take some months before your church body catches the vision that children are the future church. That may be part of the reason God has called you to the children's ministry, to heighten an awareness that children are an essential part of the kingdom of God—our future generation—building the church of Jesus Christ. So, regardless of the size of your ministry, stop, pray, and write out your reason for your ministry's existence. You will never regret having taken the time to determine where you are going and why you are going there.

At this point, take a few moments to pray and work on your philosophy of children's ministry. Use the space on the following page to develop your thoughts.

God may have called you just so you can heighten people's awareness that children are part of God's kingdom.

Turning the key: My philosophy of children's ministry is . . .

____

____

____

____

____

____

____

____

____

Ideas for my logo might include:

RECRUITMENT 2

ASSESS

your personnel needs

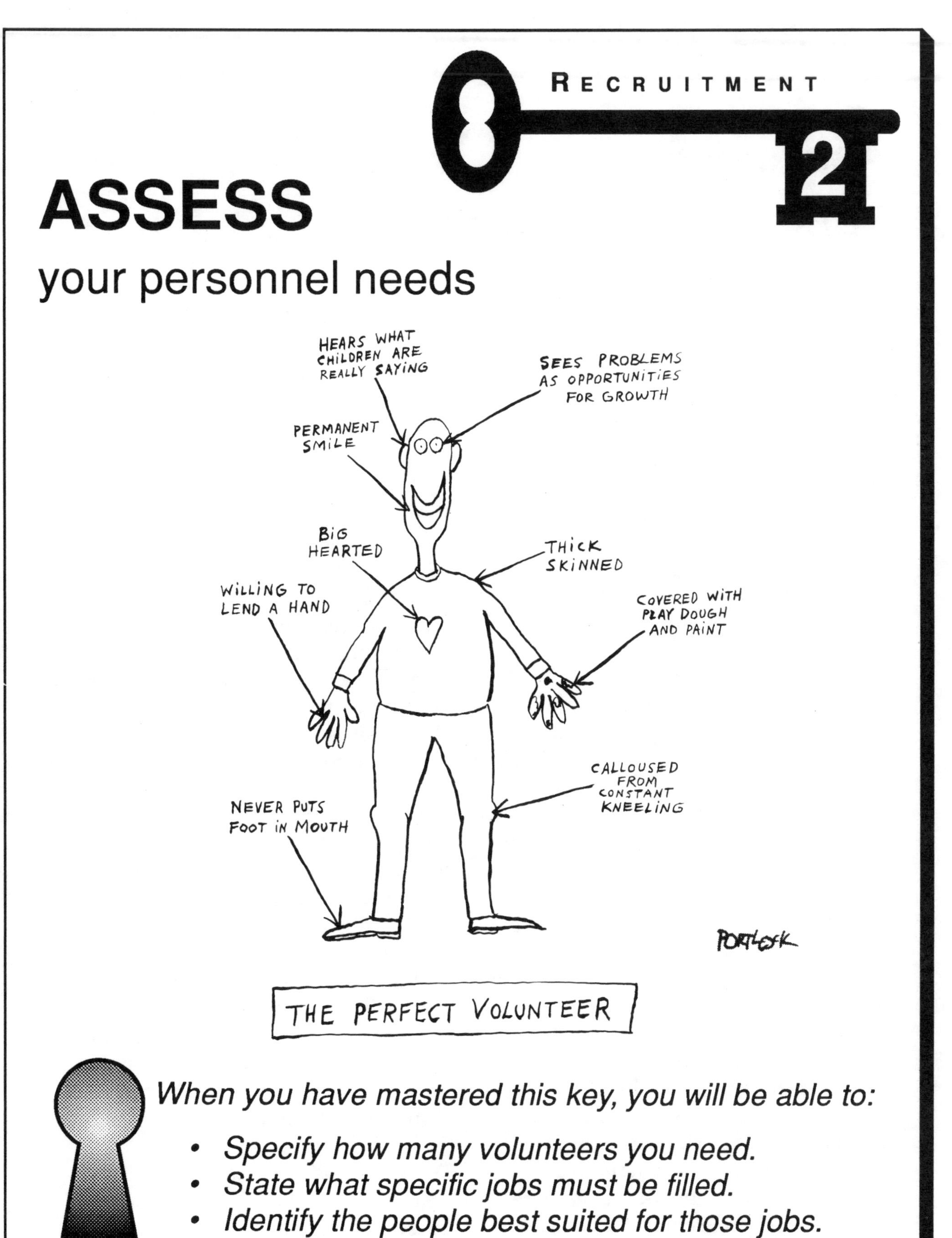

THE PERFECT VOLUNTEER

When you have mastered this key, you will be able to:

- *Specify how many volunteers you need.*
- *State what specific jobs must be filled.*
- *Identify the people best suited for those jobs.*
- *Avoid futile recruiting efforts and early burnout.*

Assessing Your Personnel Needs

The Sunday school is, without a doubt, the most substantial volunteer ministry in the church. Yet many Sunday schools constantly face the dilemma of teacher shortages and frequent turnovers. Sometimes it isn't even clear how many or what kind of volunteers are needed; too often Christian education directors and superintendents just seem to be looking for "a few more warm bodies."

There is a better way!

Determine Your Precise Needs

How can you tell what your precise needs are? The best gauge is the actual attendance of each class or club. Without this, you might respond to a need for "more help" with another volunteer, when the real need is for better training, different curriculum, or something else.

If you are not currently taking attendance, begin this week to do so in each individual classroom! Whether it's a midweek program, Sunday morning, or Sunday evening—to determine staff needs—you must begin taking attendance. If the only thing you are able to get is a head count, then by all means get it. If you are in a summer break, without classes or clubs meeting, you may need to use some alternative steps to check out your attendance. Perhaps you will need to telephone the teachers to ask for an approximate count of last years' attendance. Once you begin taking regular attendance, you may discover you don't need as many volunteers as you thought you did.

Make copies of the "Class Profile" form (Resource I-2A) to be filled out for each class. When you have discovered the real needs in each room, you will find the "Needs at a Glance Chart" (Resource I-2B) helpful. Adapt and fill out a separate chart for each program you oversee: Sunday school, children's church, club, vacation Bible school, etc. The "blank spots" will show you the positions you need to fill. Then consider the following keys to determining your current personnel needs.

Determine your desired student/teacher ratio. Once you have found the average attendance for each class, determine your desired ratio of children to adults. A general rule of thumb is to have one adult to three children under eighteen months of age, one adult to five children from eighteen to thirty-six months, one adult to six children from four years through first grade, and one adult to eight children from second through sixth grade.

Be sensitive to class size. As classes near their capacity, be alert to parents' sensitivity to over-crowded classrooms. When parents sense the room is "way

There *is* a way to escape the "always looking for a few warm bodies" syndrome.

too full," they will be hesitant to bring their child again, especially in preschool. Personal attention to the individual child is key to his or her security and comfort in the classroom. This secure feeling leads to an openness to learning. When adult classes become over-crowded, people can adapt, or choose not to attend any longer. Children do not have that option. They are brought to church by their parents, friends, relatives, or sent on a bus.

Children become confused and insecure in an over-crowded situation. Our goal is to build in them a feeling of trust. We are teaching them from the moment they enter the church grounds about the love of Jesus. Their experience should be one that lays the foundation for a trusting relationship with the Lord Jesus as well as the church.

Watch your classrooms closely so you can plan ahead for room space. As your ministry grows, you will be searching out every possible square foot for class space, but keep in mind the ideal class size and divide as necessary. Be creative—don't view over-crowding as a problem—view it as an opportunity to share God's love with more children.

Estimate room size. In addition to taking attendance, it will be of utmost importance for you to know the size of each classroom in terms of square feet of space. State and local building and safety codes will vary on the space allowance in terms of square feet per child. But most educators suggest the following: thirty to thirty-five square feet per child for birth to five years old, twenty-five square feet per child for grades one through six. These figures are, of course, the ideal. Most of us minister in situations that are not ideal, and we often have to adjust to the resources we have.

As God enables you, educate your congregation and the church board to the needs of children. This will help you as you seek to put the children of your church in the best learning atmosphere you possibly can.

Develop Job Descriptions

Consider all jobs. Make a list of all the jobs in your church's children's ministry. Start with the obvious ones like department leader (if your church is large), lead teacher, team teacher, substitute teacher, and classroom helper.

The difficulties we had in in our church in terms of recruiting volunteers caused us to think creatively to find alternative solutions to some of our recruitment problems. One creative approach is to assign some of the tasks that normally fall to the Sunday school teacher to others. People who might not

Once you begin taking regular attendance, you may discover you don't need as many volunteers as you thought you did.

want the full responsibility of teaching are often more receptive if they are assigned a specialized task. Make it sound fun, because it is!

Prepare job descriptions. Once you've listed all the positions you need to fill, the next step is to prepare a job description for each one. A sample teacher's job description that you can use as a guide for creating the others you need appears in Resource I-7C. Here are a few of the other job descriptions you might develop:

• Department leader—The primary purpose of this important function is to lead a group of teachers to a unity of spirit. This person needs to give direction and guidance to his or her department (e.g., all preschool classes). He or she is to see that curriculum is used to the fullest and that sound doctrine is taught within each classroom. This person should also be involved in leading regular training for teachers in the department; finding substitutes when needed; coordinating other helpers for snacks, crafts, song time; coordinating room arrangements, schedules and materials, etc. Churches with three or more classes in any department should consider having department leaders. They can make the life of a superintendent, children's pastor, or director so much easier. In some situations, the department leader can also be a teacher.

• Class secretary—Someone to keep records and assist in "clerical" functions. This person could take responsibility for making all name tags for each child and adult in the classroom. Some duties could include taking roll, mailing out "welcome" cards to newcomers, mailing birthday cards to students from the entire teaching staff, keeping the supplies in the room in neat order, and mailing "we missed you" cards to absentees. Secretaries in preschool classes could also set up personal shoe boxes, bins, or cubby holes for each child. Such organizers can collect take-home papers, craft work, and notices to parents so they will not be lost when the children go home. (Be sure extra organizers are avaliable for visitors.) Removing this kind of detail work from the teacher's job description greatly relieves him or her to be more available to minister to the children. When considering class secretaries, look for people who enjoy children, but don't necessarily feel comfortable "teaching."

• Bulletin board committee—A group of people to assist teachers in creating bulletin boards. If the teacher is planning a bulletin board that involves students, it is a real help to have clean paper and border put up in advance. A committee of four to six people that love

As God enables you, educate your congregation and the church board to the needs of children.

to decorate, or just be of service, can keep the rooms fresh and alive for the students. In my personal experience, I found the bulletin boards the greatest strain on the individual teacher—yet teachers want fresh, seasonal boards for their children. If you go this route, you'll need to provide resources: Rolls of colored butcher paper, lettering, borders, and bulletin board pictures can be purchased at most school supply stores.

• Supply shopper—Someone to purchase necessary supplies can be a real asset to your ministry. The ideal situation would be to have a resource room filled with the basic supples that are needed when working with kids—glue, scissors, construction paper, and so forth. It's amazing how these things can "disappear" during the course of the year. Teachers have need nearly every week of creative supplies that take a little more ingenuity to locate. I'm thinking of green cotton balls, colored macaroni, walnut shell halves, purple pipe cleaners, or stickers of animals or Bible characters.

I'm sure you can find someone in your congregation who loves to shop or loves to find bargains—that's the person for you! Hours of your time will be freed up for creative planning as you shift these kinds of jobs to the willing volunteer. People who can't help out on Sunday morning or Wednesday night can still be involved in children's ministry.

• Craft coordinator—Someone to assist teachers in making handiwork. This person could assemble one copy of the week's craft for various teachers in advance of the class. He or she could also be on hand during the class time to help the children with crafts.

• Music leader—Let's face it, not all of us are musically inclined! But leading children in song is a task that can be easily delegated to someone who is. This person could accompany singing during opening or closing exercises. In other situations, this individual could rotate to various classes throughout the hour to lead singing.

• Room resource person—You recognize the clutter. You want to get those cupboards cleaned out, the lost and found hauled away, the broken toys discarded, the old plastic flowers tossed, and torn books replaced, but you never seem to get around to it. Then consider assigning a volunteer.

All the ministry positions I've listed here can be a real help to you and your teachers in carrying out your goals and philosophy. Begin by picking one position you'd like to add, develop a job description, and go for it!

People who can't help out
on Sunday morning or Wednesday night
can still be involved in children's ministry.

Turning the key: The classes with the greatest needs are . . .

Class: ________________ Need: ____________________

Class: ________________ Need: ____________________

Class: ________________ Need: ____________________

New ministry positions I want to add are . . .

Position: ______________ Date to find person by: ________

Position: ______________ Date to find person by: ________

Position: ______________ Date to find person by: ________

RECRUITMENT 3

SEEK

God's guidance through prayer

"I guess I shouldn't have skipped key #3."

When you have mastered this key, you will be able to:

- *Pray with more confidence that God will answer.*
- *Pray with much greater focus and perseverance.*
- *Create a prayer requests/prayer answers log.*

think about "prayer pages"

Praying for Your Children's Ministry

Saying, "Pray about it," may seem like trite advice to some people. But that's exactly what Jesus told us to do in Luke 10:2: "The harvest is plentiful, but the workers are few. Ask the Lord of the harvest, therefore, to send out workers into his harvest field."

My attitude about praying for volunteers for the children's ministry has changed recently. I began to see that God is faithful! As I reflect over the last ten years in children's ministry, I'm aware that God has never—not even once—failed to bring the people the children needed to minister to them.

My Personal Experience

As I began my ministry to children many years ago, it was a stretching experience for me far beyond anything I had ever dreamed possible. I thought I was going to "help out a little" at church because there was a need. Little did I realize the way in which God was going to show Himself strong on my behalf (II Chron. 16:9, KJV). The Lord is so gracious to us in not allowing us to see what is ahead on our spiritual journey. He gently guides us, leads us, and supplies our needs. Each new challenge that comes will give you the opportunity to pray and see God answer. Begin where you are now. Face each need with the Lord as your partner. One by one He will supply the need—I assure you! Yes, wouldn't it be wonderfully exhilarating to have a waiting list of people to work with our children? Perhaps one day there will be. But take one day at a time; look at this coming Sunday. What are your specific needs this week? Faithfully, ever so faithfully, God will meet your needs.

Pray with the hearts of those little children before you and before the Lord. They are His. He loves them so much more than we could ever dream of loving them. It is our goal to impact their lives for eternity. We should pray to this end. God sees the future. God knows where every teacher and every child is in their spiritual walk with Him. His blend of those teachers and children will be perfect as we pray to find His selection of children's ministry people.

After I began my ministry to children, God allowed one of my own to be taken home to Him. My oldest child, Mike, was murdered at the age of seventeen. Suddenly, the little smudge-faced boys, those little curly-headed girls, all the children before me, took on new significance. When you pray for recruits, for people that will be ministering directly with the children, pray for those whose hearts are teachable. Children will be teaching and molding the adults' lives, as well as the teachers molding and teaching the children. Keep praying for God to supply your needs. He knows

Prayer is the constant awareness that the Lord is ever present with us.

exactly what those needs are. He knows every child's individual need, and He alone will be able to meet those needs. Pray! Pray! Pray! He will answer.

Pray without Ceasing

Begin to think of your entire day as communion with God. He is with you every moment and as He guides you through each week. Be aware that He will bring certain people to your mind and across your way. Throughout the day ask Him to prepare hearts for His work, particularly at times prior to doing some major telephoning or a recruitment campaign. When the Lord brings to your mind those He would direct you to, ask God to prepare you for the ideal opportunity to talk to them.

Practice His personal presence. Prayer is the constant awareness that the Lord is ever present with us. It is the awesome perception that I have been infused with God Himself.

Keep a log of your prayer requests. Record God's answers as He brings person after person to fill the needs. In times of discouragement, you can return to your list and be encouraged by remembering God's past faithfulness. The person you think would be the least likely to be working with children may be just the one God has a place for in your ministry. Photocopy Resource I-3A to begin creating a Prayer Log for recording your prayer requests. Punch holes as indicated to preserve your Prayer Log in a three-ring binder.

Be specific when you pray. Call out to God each individual class or club. "I need two leaders for Adventure Club in the primary grades!" "There is a need, Lord, for a new nursery supervisor, show me who it is to be." Be sure the entries in your Prayer Log are specific.

Seek out persons of prayer to pray with you about specific needs. It is so encouraging to be able to depend on someone to pray with you regarding a serious need—possibly someone you could meet with each week. Ask the Lord for a diligent partner, a person who loves children and would pray earnestly for their needs to be met. Share with this person copies of your Prayer Log. (When needs arise in different classrooms, you may also want to call the parents, and ask them to pray with you about what teachers and helpers God would bring into their child's classroom.)

Give God the Glory For Answered Prayer

When needs are filled, be sure to shout it from the rooftops. God gives us

People love to hear about answered prayer. They also love to be the answers to those prayers!

a command to praise Him on many occasions in His Word (Ps. 106:1). Giving Him the glory is why we live.

Psalm 34:1 is a verse that would be good for each of us in children's ministry to memorize. It so aptly states what we want to portray to the children to whom we minister. "I will extol the Lord at all times; his praise will always be on my lips."

Children's pastors, directors of Christian education, and Sunday school superintendents are often viewed by their congregations as always crying about the needs of children's ministry. Let's change that image by being quick to praise God when needs are filled. People love to hear about answered prayer. They also love to be the answers to those prayers! Letting those who volunteer know that you believe they are God's answer to prayer will reinforce their joyful sense of being in God's will.

Meditate on each Scripture in the box below, writing a sentence about how it applies to your search for volunteers.

Turning the key . . .

II Chronicles 6:40 ______________________________

____

Psalm 17:6 ______________________________

____

Matthew 21:22 ______________________________

____

Acts 1:14 ______________________________

____

Colossians 4:2-4 ______________________________

____

I Peter 3:12 ______________________________

____

RECRUITMENT

4

ENLIST

a team of dedicated recruiters

"The new uniforms might confuse people, but to me you're all number one!"

When you have mastered this key, you will be able to:

- *Find a team of helpers who care.*
- *Inspire them to help in the recruiting process.*
- *Equip them to locate new volunteers.*

Let People Know That Recruiting Is Everybody's Job!

I don't need to tell you how impossible it is to recruit everyone you need all by yourself, even though most of the people in your congregation may think that it *is* possible. What's even more discouraging is that some probably think that you should do it alone. After all, that's your job! If you are serving in a volunteer capacity, everyone thinks you are there because you have some special gift of recruitment. Why else would anyone volunteer for such a job? If you are a paid staff person, then of course: "That's what you get paid for."

Don't Overlook the Obvious

But since you can't do the whole job by yourself, you need help. And the best option for rallying assistance is to involve your current children's ministry team in the job of recruiting new volunteers. Statistics suggest that most recruiting efforts for volunteers are about 10 percent effective. That means that if you need one new person, you'll have to talk to ten. If you need ten, you'll have to contact a hundred. Of course, it isn't always that difficult. If you are in a small church where you know everyone, and people are not already overextended, you might be very selective with whom you speak. Your ratio might go up. On the other hand, effectiveness is sometimes even less than 10 percent. Either way, it doesn't take long to see that if you need twenty or even more new volunteers, the job of finding them is far too large for one person. Therefore, make the entire staff aware that recruitment is everybody's job.

Enhancing 'Ownership' Of the Ministry

Dr. Dennis E. Williams, of Denver Seminary, says that "motivation is the ability to get people to do what you want because they want to do it." So how are you going to accomplish that task among your current volunteers? How can you inspire them to willingly pitch in finding more volunteers?

Help your staff "own" their classes. The volunteers who work with you in children's ministry need to feel ownership of their class. As they begin to minister to a certain group of children, those children will become "their" children. It is much like the parent in his or her home. When parents feel they lack certain skills or tools to give the best to their child, they go out and seek what they need to do to become better parents or to give the child more personal attention. These teachers will be the same way. As you share with them their responsibility in training and nurturing those children, they will catch the vision of "I need to recruit."

The best option for rallying assistance is to involve your current teachers in the job of recruiting.

O— *Ask each teacher to complete a "Dream Sheet"* (Resource I-4A) concerning what he or she would like to be doing with his or her class in six months if there were no limitations. Discuss these ideas with each teacher, comparing the teacher's ideas with the "Class Profile" (Resource I-2A) which you created earlier for that class. Talk about the ideal teacher/student ratio and class size. Make plans together.

O— *Build team spirit*. Yes, the volunteers are working for the Lord—their primary motivation. Yet when they know they are not out there all alone, they feel affirmed and work harder.

Once you have effectively helped your volunteers "own" the overall children's ministry, you can share with them the statistics on recruitment and they will more easily see that it is an impossible task for any one person to accomplish alone. In this way you transfer a share of the burden for recruitment to others—a team that can provide informed and effective help.

Building a team spirit among your children's ministry volunteers is of utmost importance. These dedicated workers are perhaps the least encouraged of any in the church. It normally is not a ministry that is "up front." Cuddling babies, changing diapers, and helping with finger paints may seem to many to be of little value, And the responses we receive from the children may be a long time in coming. So it is helpful for our volunteers to know they are on a special team.

Let them all know the numbers of people ministering to children. Those ministering on Sunday morning may not have any idea that there is a whole crew of people working on Wednesday or Sunday evening. It is helpful for them to see the bigger picture and know exactly how many children's workers there are. When the choir gets up to sing, it's easy to see how many people are in it. However, if you work in the nursery or children's church, you may only see those in your department.

Some suggestions for helping volunteers "feel" the team spirit include:

- Sharing your recruitment philosophy with them,
- Using a theme verse for the year that all are encouraged to memorize and apply,
- Giving everyone a special pin or button that identifies them as part of the children's ministry team,
- Sharing total attendance figures and other newsworthy items.

Other suggestions for building team spirit will be included in the chapters that follow.

When volunteers know
they aren't out there all alone,
they feel affirmed and work harder.

Turning the key:

Plan here how you will share your recruitment philosophy at your next meeting: ____________________

____

____

____

What verse could be your theme verse for the year? __________

____

____

Write down the first step you can take to build team spirit among your staff: ____________________

____

____

____

RECRUITMENT 5

DEVELOP

a parent-helper program

"I appreciate your signing up to be a parent-helper, Mr. Bloom—but could you give us a little less parent and a little more helper?"

When you have mastered this key, you will be able to:

- *Set up a "Parent of the Week" program.*
- *Bring parents into the classroom as helpers.*
- *Delegate responsibility for this program to others.*

How to Involve Parents In Supporting the Children's Ministry

In addition to the formal teachers and helpers you recruit for your children's ministry, it is often desirable to have additional helpers and substitutes in reserve. One good way to enlist auxiliary help is to develop a parent-helper program that is based in the individual classes and managed by the teachers, freeing you from this administrative task. But first, you will have to set up the program and equip the teachers with a plan to accomplish it.

When parents visit their children's classrooms, most are surprised at how much teaching and learning goes on within the Sunday school or midweek program. Many will enjoy seeing what their children are learning and experiencing in the classroom so much that they will be glad to help out on an irregular basis as needed. However, this positive response will only happen when parents find the classroom to be smooth-running and pleasant. Parents won't want to come back to chaotic classrooms. So start with those classes that are well-organized even if it seems like you need the most help elsewhere.

Launch a 'Parent of the Week' Program

Each week have the selected classes name their "Parent of the Week" for the coming week's class or club. This can be by random selection such as drawing names from a hat, or by following some preassigned order. (See Resource I-5A.) If the children are old enough, invitations can be sent home with them. (See Resource I-5B.) Otherwise, the teacher should mail the invitations. The teacher or leader should then contact the parent during the week to be sure the invitation was received and that the he or she will be able to attend the class. This also gives the teacher or club leader an opportunity to find out if this is a single-parent home. We want to assure those who are single parents that they are as much a part of this program as those from two-parent homes.

When the parent arrives the next week, a special place should be provided for him or her to sit. This could be a special place with decorations, or a seat under a banner that says "Parent of the Week." Time should also be taken to introduce the parent to the class. In my own church, many of our parents were so impressed with what went on in the classroom, they found it easy to say yes when asked to be a parent-helper at a later date. There is great value in having each teacher call the parents personally. Teachers will get to know the parents of their students and build more meaningful relationships with the student and the parent, after a personal contact.

The main purpose of each parent's visit is to observe what is happening in

Parents won't want to come back to chaotic classrooms. So start with those that are well-organized.

his or her child's Sunday school class and to enhance the child's self-esteem by having a family member present and honored. But this step of familiarization is essential preparation to inviting the parents back as helpers.

Utilize Interested Parents

Once several parents have visited the classroom as a "Parent of the Week," the teacher can determine which ones would be most suited to helping in the classroom. Many parents will have other responsibilities in the church that prevent them from being regular or long-term helpers.

However, the parents that are able to help in their child's class will need to know they are really needed. When a parent comes to class as a helper, the teacher should have the morning schedule written out with the specific things he or she wants the parent to do. For example, at 9:00 AM the parent-helper will assist at the puzzle table, at 9:30 AM aid with crafts, or set out juice and crackers. The more specific you make the instructions, the better.

Any person feels inadequate if he or she doesn't know what to do once in the class. The helpers will also feel that they are not really needed if the teachers do all the work and just let them stand around wondering why they are there. The teachers need to let the parents know they are needed by putting them right to work!

Getting Started

The following keys should help you get started in involving the parents.

Determine which classes are appropriate for parent-helpers, and use the space at the end of this section to list them. List the teachers' names, and call them this week. Remember, the classes you start with need to be basically orderly.

Provide instructions for the participating teachers. Photocopy the "Parent of the Week Program" instruction sheet (Resource I-5A) and distribute it to the teachers you want to start the program.

Supply "Parent of the Week" invitations for the teachers to use by adapting and/or photocopying Resource I-5B.

Fold each sheet in quarters to create an openable card. Encourage the children in the classes to personalize the cards by coloring them. If they are old enough and the class is small, they might also sign their names on the inside blank page.

On the following page, list some of your ideas for getting a Parent of the Week program started. Be specific in terms of age and class.

Teachers need to let parents know
they are needed
by putting them right to work!

Turning the key:

Date we will begin a "Parent of the Week" program:____________

Best place(s) to start:

Teacher: ______________________________

Teacher: ______________________________

Teacher: ______________________________

Teacher: ______________________________

Ideas to share with teachers on how to best use parent-helpers:

____

____

____

____

____

____

RECRUITMENT 6

LAUNCH

a church-wide recruitment campaign

"Something tells me we're going to be asked to volunteer this morning."

When you have mastered this key, you will be able to:

- *Refine and define what needs still exist.*
- *Select a recruitment theme.*
- *Present the joys of children's ministry.*
- *Make personal contact with interested persons.*

Launching a Church-Wide Campaign

Together we have looked at some of the basic things that need to be done before we begin an all-out campaign to recruit the volunteers we need into the children's ministry. Let's review the keys we have discussed.

With Recruitment . . .
🔑 **1**, you established your philosophy for children's ministry.
🔑 **2**, you determined your personnel needs.
🔑 **3**, you sought God's guidance through prayer.
🔑 **4**, your existing teachers gained a burden for helping to staff their own classes.
🔑 **5**, several classes inaugurated the parent-helper program.

Select a Recruitment Theme

Now it is time to think of a theme for the year. If you have never used a theme before you will find it really helpful. A theme will motivate your volunteers in their thinking. Somehow, when we use a verse of Scripture or even a slogan it has a cohesiveness that draws people together. Most of your best slogans will come from Scripture. The Lord will be so gracious in helping you be creative as you wait before Him to help you decide the direction you want to go. Here are a few suggestions to get you started:

- Bear fruit, fruit that will last (John 15:16).
- 85 percent (When people ask, "What's 85 percent?" you can reply that 85 percent of all Christian conversions occur between the ages of four and fourteen according to Lionel Hunt in *Handbook of Children's Evangelism* [Moody Press].)
- Let the children come to Jesus.
- "Who Will Teach the Children?" (David C. Cook Publishing Co. offers a complete recruitment video and resource guide that poses this question in a very poignant manner. The resource guide gives step-by-step instructions for a campaign entitled, "I Will!" It includes helpful suggestions for using the video in a variety of settings and contains a number of reproducible resources like buttons, fliers, posters, and much more. It's available from your local Christian bookstore or David C. Cook Publishing Co.)
- Bind it to their foreheads (Deut. 6:6, 7).
- K-I-D-S (This is an acrostic for "Kids Invite Dedicated Servants".)
- The harvest is plentiful (Matthew 9:37).
- Just say "Yes!"

It's a good idea to keep your theme short and to the point. This way people

A theme will motivate
your volunteers in their thinking.

will easily remember it. Let your creative juices flow. Get together with a couple other people. Prime your pumps by studying the elements of good slogans. Then brainstorm by writing down everything that comes to mind. When you have several ideas, begin refining them.

Plan Your Campaign

A church-wide campaign once a year is a great way to make opportunities in children's ministry known to your congregation. You may want to hold your campaign on three consecutive Sundays. But it will be important to have everything planned in advance.

Saturate the entire church body with your theme and logo. For instance:

- Use bulletin inserts with your theme as the core (Resources I-6A and Resource I-6B). Surprisingly, you may not want to list your specific needs in this initial campaign. If a person wants to teach juniors but sees you only need someone for primaries, he or she might not volunteer. On the other hand, if the invitation is general, you can talk to people about serving where the real need is until they can move into their first choice spot. Most will be willing to do this and discover the joy that comes with serving children of any age.
- Encourage all current children's ministry staff and volunteers to wear badges or ribbons with the theme. (See Resource I-6C.)
- Display a large banner on the church grounds with your theme and logo.

Schedule Sunday morning presentations. After creating curiosity with your theme and logo, give some substance to your campaign.

- During the morning worship service on each of the three campaign Sundays, arrange for a testimony by one of your current volunteers. Choose people who are articulate and enthusiastic about ministry.
- One Sunday you may want to use the video, "Who Will Teach the Children?" that was mentioned earlier.
- A slide presentation of children's faces from your own ministry programs always warms the heart of people. Use appropriate background music and automatic frame forward for a professional touch.
- A skit by some of the teachers would also be a great tool for telling others about the needs in children's ministry.

After creating curiosity with your theme and logo, give some substance to your campaign.

Provide opportunities for people to ask questions and get information. Some ways to do this might be:

- Erect a children's ministry booth decorated with crepe paper and balloons to heighten visiblity. Staff the booth with current volunteers. Have extra bulletin inserts on hand (Resources I-6A and I-6B) which people can use to indicate their interest. While people are on their way to Sunday school or worship, you may want to have a slide projector (or video) running that constantly shows images of your entire children's ministry. People (especially parents) love to see pictures of children in action. It also gives those that don't know much about the children's ministry an opportunity to see what's going on with the children.
- Send people to the adult Sunday school classes all three Sundays to share the special blessings received working with children.
- If you have a church newsletter, publish letters from children telling how important their Sunday school teacher or club leader is.
- Telephone all prospects within a week, or otherwise talk personally. Some people need a personal invitation to dispel the fears they have about working with children. *Listen* to their questions, feelings, and experiences. Encourage but don't coerce. The Holy Spirit will give you the right people whose lives will be enriched by their ministry.

Turning the key: Planning your campaign.

Possible theme(s): ______________________________

____

____

Date of campaign: ______________________________

People (especially parents)
love to see pictures of children in action.

Ideas for worship:

Date: ________ Idea: ______________________________

Date: ________ Idea: ______________________________

Date: ________ Idea: ______________________________

Volunteers to give testimonies in adult Sunday school:

Class: ____________ Volunteer: ______________________

Class: ____________ Volunteer: ______________________

Class: ____________ Volunteer: ______________________

Volunteers to work the children's ministry booth:

Date: ________ Volunteers: __________________________

Date: ________ Volunteers: __________________________

Date: ________ Volunteers: __________________________

Other ideas for a successful campaign: ____________________

____

____

RECRUITMENT 7

PREPARE

for when people say 'Yes'

"No, the concert is down the street. This is the VBS volunteer sign-up line."

When you have mastered this key, you will be able to:

- *Provide an introductory packet to new volunteers.*
- *Match volunteers' strengths with positions.*
- *Introduce volunteers to the desired age group.*
- *Build ministry teams for effective partnerships.*

How to Respond When People Volunteer

One of the most important factors in placing volunteers into your ministry will be their comfort and security in knowing they are not being put into a classroom for a life sentence. Let them know from the very outset that you are their friend. They should understand that your goal is for each child to be a priority in the children's ministry. One of the best ways to achieve that goal is for the volunteers to clearly understand their role in that process.

When a volunteer says yes, or if a person has expressed interest and wants to know more, what should be your first response? The first thing they will want to know is what you expect from them. What does this job entail? How long are they expected to serve? Who are the students? How will they know what to do?

Get Ready, Get Set . . .

The following keys will help unlock the mystery of children's ministry to the first-time volunteer:

Provide a "Volunteers Packet." When a person expresses an interest in becoming involved in children's ministry, a helpful "get acquainted" tool is a Volunteers Ministry Packet. The information it contains will largely depend on your church's requirements (e.g., church membership, born-again believer, baptism, etc.). This packet might contain several of the following:

- A welcome letter (use or adapt Resource I-7A).
- The personal information sheet (Resource I-7B).
- A job description (Resource I-7C).
- Your church doctrinal statement.
- Your philosophy of children's ministry.
- A yearly schedule of staff meetings and/or in-service training dates.
- A covenant to sign (adapt Resource I-7D, filling in the length of service and contact person spaces).
- Any other material you want them to read or have at their disposal (e.g., resources on discipline, leading a child to Christ, building self-esteem in children, etc. The book for the appropriate age level in the "Successful Teaching Series" by Dr. Larry Richards—available from David C. Cook Publishing Co.—would make an excellent addition, also from the same publisher, *I Love Sunday School* by Joseph Bayly.

A handy way to package these papers is in a self-sealing clear plastic bag. You may want to enlarge your logo and have it reproduced on an 8 $^{1}/_{2}$" x 11" sheet as a cover page for the packet. The

The first thing they will want to know is what you expect from them.

new volunteers can begin reading through the material to gain some idea of what you will be expecting of them. Ask them to fill out the enclosed forms and make an appointment to meet with them in the near future.

Arrange a personal interview. After you've delivered the packet, set a time to talk face-to-face. As you review the forms, this information will help you discuss the volunteers' strengths and/or any problem areas you might see. Also encourage them to ask questions. During this interview you should explain the overall structure of your children's ministry, to whom they are responsible, and the general schedule for the coming year (e.g., staff and training meetings). This may also be the time to provide any curriculum or teaching materials the volunteer will use.

The most important thing coming from this interview will be your ministry to that volunteer. Yes, you are the person overseeing the ministry to children. But remember, the volunteer will be the one touching, loving, and reaching the children. You are the motivating force for them when the trench ministry becomes difficult. When volunteers know there is a person directing the ministry, their confidence soars! When they know that person is their friend and mentor, they feel the Lord's confidence to step into the lives of children!

It's also important to discuss expectations. A one-year commitment is not impossible. The more we expect from people, the more we get from them. In this area of ministry in particular, consistency in being with children every week is important to help them feel comfortable and secure.

. . . Go!

Now it's time to get him or her into the classroom. But even this stage can have several helpful steps.

Let volunteers observe in the classroom. Following your personal interview, have volunteers go into a classroom to observe. Most of the time we need them so much they end up going into the classroom to help, but a day of observation would be most helpful to them. If they do not know what age-group they wish to minister to, they would need to observe in more than one room to gain a feel for different ages.

Build ministry teams. Now you are ready to assign volunteers to a classroom. Never put a new volunteer into a classroom alone. They need to be part of a team. Ideally, it's best to pair a new volunteer with an experienced teacher. If this can't happen in every situation, each volunteer should be teamed with

The more we expect from people,
the more we get from them.
A full-year commitment is not unreasonable.

at least one other person. Even in the smallest classroom of children, they need to have a partner in ministry with them. Teaching teams can support one another in planning; one can teach and the other help quiet children or provide a comforting lap; the class can be divided for certain activities; crafts often need more adult hands to help; etc.

It is also best for safety reasons not to have a person alone. In every situation there is a possibility of emergency. You need one person to stay in the classroom and one to go for help. A partner in the classroom for every teacher and helper is not only supportive, but a necessity.

Turning the key: List the things you consider important to include in a volunteers' packet . . .

I need to prepare:

- ❑ Welcome letter
- ❑ Job description(s)
- ❑ Doctrinal statement
- ❑ Resource book
- ❑ My philosophy of children's ministry
- ❑ Personal information sheet
- ❑ Logo sheet and cover insert
- ❑ Yearly schedule of staff meetings

I would also like to include: ______________________________

____

____

____

RECRUITMENT 8

INITIATE

a junior-helper program

"I think she's taking this junior-helper thing a little too far."

When you have mastered this key, you will be able to:

- *Create opportunities to train future volunteers.*
- *Avoid competing with regular youth programs.*
- *Begin implementing a Junior-Helper Program.*

How to Train Future Volunteers

A volunteer resource often overlooked in churches is young people sixth grade and older. Not only are many junior and senior high young people capable of providing valuable help with younger children, but this is a golden opportunity to begin training them for future ministry in the church.

Two Words of Advice

Work with your youth programs. A well-organized Junior-Helper Program will enhance, not take away from your youth ministry. It has a two-fold purpose: to train young people for future ministry and to build character and responsibility within the young teens of your church. As you work along side the person in charge of the youth program, he or she will become excited about the growth visible among the youth as they begin to minister and care for others.

There are many opportunities within your church structure to use youth as helpers. You will probably find this program most eagerly desired by sixth grade and junior high students. But in some programs within the children's ministry, the high school kids will want to actively participate—midweek programs, summer day camps, vacation Bible school, children's choir programs, children's church—literally anywhere you need good volunteers.

Set an age limit and stick to it. Junior-Helpers should be youth in sixth grade or above. Using children any younger than this will often hamper the teacher, not help him or her. Be firm on the age, even though it's difficult to say no to an eager young person that wants to help.

Working with young people involves working with their parents as well. Parents of a mature fifth grader may call and say, "My daughter really wants to work with the children. She is very mature and we would like to have her help in a classroom." It may be true that this child is capable of working with little ones, but if you let one fourth or fifth grader work, you will have to let others help that are not mature, often causing the teacher more annoyance than genuine help. You can be firm about your age limit, but say encouragingly, "We are really looking forward to your daughter being a Junior-Helper as soon as she is in sixth grade."

Training for the Future

Emphasize the Junior-Helper Program as a training experience. The young people involved should understand that this is not an escape from worship. Approach them with the idea

Working with young people involves working with their parents as well. They, too, must make a commitment.

that they will be in training for future years of service for the Lord. A Junior-Helper Program can be something children begin looking forward to as they approach sixth grade—a privilege that comes with age!

Some keys to implement this program would be as follows:

🗝 *Prepare a job description* for the Junior-Helper (see Resource I-8A for a sample).

🗝 *Talk with your teachers* about their role in this program—they play an integral part in making this program a success (see Resource I-8B). Be sure teachers desire or are willing to have a Junior-Helper before placement. (Junior-Helpers, depending on their age and maturity, should be used primarily in preschool classrooms. Older junior high and senior high youth can be used in early elementary age, as well as preschool.)

🗝 *Advertise* the availability of this program in the church bulletin or newsletter.

🗝 *When young people contact you,* respond with a telephone call to discuss their interest and check the authenticity of their commitment. It's also wise to discuss the young person's involvement in the Junior-Helper Program with his or her parents. It will be as much a commitment of the parents as it will be of the young person. It is often the parent who gets the Junior-Helper to the church early and regularly.

🗝 *Mail a letter of expectations* to prospective Junior-Helpers (see Resource I-8A) so both the young people and their parents can see it in writing. This will eliminate any confusion regarding what is expected from the Junior-Helpers.

🗝 *At the same time mail a memo* (Resource I-8B) to the teachers or department leaders so they will know which young person will be coming into their room to serve as a Junior-Helper. The letter should include what you expect from the teacher as well. You may want to telephone the teacher a few days later to see if there are any questions about the plan.

🗝 *Give a teacher's guide to each Junior-Helper,* so he or she can be aware of what Scripture and story will be discussed in the classroom each Sunday.

On the next page list the children's ministries in your church that could benefit from some Junior-Helpers.

Be sure teachers desire
or are willing to have a Junior-Helper
before placement.

Turning the key:

These children's ministries could benefit from a Junior-Helper

Program: ____

____

____

The date I'd like to begin a Junior-Helper Program: ____________

The age requirement I've decided on is: ____________________

The teachers I will approach first with the idea are: ____________

____

____

Some youth who might make good Junior-Helpers are: ________

____

____

____

RECRUITMENT

9

CHAMPION

children's ministry as the place to be

"I'm sure I'll get my money's worth this year—I'm teaching the 5th and 6th graders."

When you have mastered this key, you will be able to:

- *Lift up the vision of welcoming children for Jesus' sake.*
- *Ask people to volunteer without apologizing.*
- *Substitute positive phrases for negative ones.*

How to Promote a Positive Spirit About Children's Ministry

"The concept of childhood, so vital to the traditional American way of life," says David Elkind in *The Hurried Child,* "is threatened with extinction in the society we have created. Today's child has become the unwilling, unintended victim of overwhelming stress—the stress borne of rapid, bewildering social change and constantly rising expectations. The contemporary parent dwells in a pressure-cooker of competing demands, transitions, role changes, personal and professional uncertainties over which he or she exerts slight direction. We seek release from stress whenever we can, and usually the one sure gambit of our control is the home. Here, if nowhere else, we enjoy the fact (or illusion) of playing a determining role. If child-rearing necessarily entails stress, then by hurrying children to grow up, or by treating them as adults, we hope to remove a portion of our burden of worry and anxiety and to enlist our children's aid in carrying life's load. We do not mean our children harm in acting thus—on the contrary, as a society we have come to imagine that it is good for young people to mature rapidly. Yet we do our children harm when we hurry them through childhood."

Children's Ministry Is the Place to Be

As followers of Jesus we have the opportunity to minister to children who are being stressed beyond belief. Even children from Christian homes are operating under stress levels we knew nothing about growing up in the thirties, forties, fifties, and sixties. The simple discipline problems of chewing gum in class, being tardy, or talking with your neighbor are no longer considered important. Parents divorcing, no one home when the child arrives from school, drug and alcohol abuse, violent crime, and child molestation—these are what children face today in epidemic proportions.

Our future leaders are in our classrooms every week—leaders who will take us into the next century. What greater privilege could we have than to share Jesus' love with little children that often go to bed at night wondering if anyone loves them? The knowledge of God's love and the strength that comes as they realize they are special people, loved and valued by God and us, will be a crucial factor in the choices they make as adults.

Children's ministry? It's the place to be! Working with children today will greatly impact not only their future but ours as well. It is undoubtedly a key ministry in the church that will be carried into the next century with lasting effects. Let the children come to Jesus!—the poor ones, the abused ones, the rich ones, the shy ones, the bratty

Ministering to children is a privilege!
If you are convinced of that,
you need to convey that reality.

ones, the spoiled ones, the "perfect ones," the mouthy ones, and every one that God allows us to touch.

Changing the Image

Unfortunately, we are often apologetic about asking people to work with children in the church. Unconsciously we convey the attitude, "If you're not doing anything else important, could you help with the children?" Why? Ministering to children is a privilege! If you are convinced of that, you need to convey that reality from every fiber of your being—by the way you walk on Sunday mornings, your smile, the inflection in your voice when you talk to others about children's ministry.

Here are a few key suggestions to help champion children's ministry:

Avoid negative phrases. Determine to never invite someone into children's ministry with a negative statement:

- "I don't suppose you could . . ."
- "You are my last hope."
- "I know it's not much fun."
- "There's no one else available."

Strike these kinds of statements from your vocabulary! If you feel someone is your "last hope," trust God to supply the "ram in the bushes," as He did for Abraham. God knows your needs.

Use positive phrases. A person who is approached about *ministering* to children will be much more responsive than one who is asked to just be a warm body in a room full of children. Phrasing your invitations in a positive way will even give you a boost when you're feeling discouraged with your job. Positive approaches might include:

- "A real blessing is in store for you with those neat fourth graders."
- "As I prayed about the need we have in kindergarten, the Lord brought you to mind as a possible person to minister in that grade."
- "Would you consider the privilege of ministering in our nursery, to love and cuddle the babies the Lord is sending to us?"
- "There is a spot in our twos and threes department that has your name on it. You'd be great!"

Remember, negatives discourage! Positive approaches recruit!

The vision for children's ministry must be heightened in the heart of people. Terminology is often a key factor. Consider changing some major vocabulary around the concept of children's ministry, for example:

- "Ministry to children" vs. "Working with kids."

Welcoming children—inviting them, hugging them, teaching them, loving them—is welcoming Jesus into our midst.

- "Children's ministry team" vs. "Children's workers."
- "Loving care" vs. "Baby-sitting."
- "Would you like to minister?" vs. "Would you be willing to work?"

Keep the focus on Jesus. When in the trenches of children's ministry, it's easy to lose focus. Ordering supplies, recruiting teachers, making lists, finding substitutes . . . what's it all about? We so often get caught up in building the ministry, we neglect the Person who is ultimately responsible for any "success." But it's important to remember our basic calling: to serve and honor the Lord. It was Jesus who said, "Whoever welcomes this little child in my name welcomes me" (Luke 9:48). Welcoming children—inviting them, hugging them, teaching them, loving them—is welcoming Jesus into our midst.

This focus can be helpful and encouraging to your volunteers. Keep it at the forefront of all you do and say.

Champion the children. But ministering to children is often viewed as minor compared to really "important" ministry. When we apologize for asking a person to be involved with the children, they receive the message that the job you're inviting them to do is secondary. But it was Jesus Himself who said, "Let the little children to come to me" (Matt. 19:14). And as for how important children are in the kingdom of God, Jesus said, "Whoever humbles himself like this child is the greatest in the kingdom of heaven" (Matt. 18:4). We need the children! We need to be with them, work with them, let them touch our lives—because they reveal to us something of God's kingdom.

But ministry to children often needs a champion, someone who keeps it before the whole congregation as a high calling. "The work we are doing for Jesus is important! Come be a part of bringing children to Him! You will find your cup of blessing filled and running over!"

Turning the key:

Write positive phrases to begin using with prospective volunteers:

____

____

Part 2

SUPPORT

CULTIVATE

the attitude of a servant

"Purple is definitely your color, Bob—but do all the teachers have to call you 'Your Majesty'?"

When you have mastered this key, you will be able to:

- *Grow in the role of serving your volunteers.*
- *Help all your volunteers experience success.*
- *Be more sensitive to your volunteers' needs.*

How to Serve Your Volunteers So They Can Be Successful

Don't ever underestimate the importance of the volunteer as you give direction to children's ministry. Without the volunteer to be your hands, feet, and voice, there would be no children's ministry. These are the people who will carry out your vision and goals for reaching boys and girls with the Gospel and love of Jesus. Not only should you offer the training and tools they need to do their job, but volunteers deserve your care, support, and encouragement.

Develop the Attitude of a Servant

An important part of your role as Sunday school superintendent or director of children's ministries is to serve the volunteers on your staff. In fact, the New Testament has much to say about this key aspect of the leader's role.

The nature of Jesus was servanthood. Think for a minute how Jesus conducted His ministry. He selected twelve disciples whom He trained in order to go out and make disciples of others; then He bowed out of the picture. As you give oversight to your church's children's ministry, you, too, will be training volunteers who in turn will be discipling the children. In teaching the Philippians about the attitudes of leaders, the apostle Paul pointed them to Christ's ministry:

> Each of you should look not only to your own interests, but also to the interests of others. Your attitude should be the same as that of Christ Jesus: Who, being in very nature God, did not consider equality with God something to be grasped, but made himself nothing, taking the very nature of a servant . . . (Phil. 2:4-11).

And Jesus Himself made it clear what attitude the disciples should have toward their coworkers:

> "Whoever wants to become great among you must be your servant, and whoever wants to be first must be your slave—just as the Son of Man did not come to be served, but to serve . . ." (Matt. 20:26-28).

Jesus taught by His own actions that godly leadership was not power and "lording it over" others but loving, humble service. Even in a time of crisis, Jesus took time to perform a humble service for His weary disciples—He washed their feet. Then He told them:

> "Now that I, your Lord and Teacher, have washed your feet, you also should wash one another's feet. I have set you an example that you should do as I have done for

Get excited about making your teachers successful!

you. I tell you the truth, no servant is greater than his master . . ." (John 13:14-16).

O—— *Serving your volunteers is serving the Lord.* Sometimes we get so busy "serving the Lord" we forget to serve each other. But in a parable about the Sheep and the Goats at the Last Judgment, Jesus made it clear that serving others *is* the way we serve Him.

> "Then the righteous will answer him, 'Lord, when did we see you hungry and feed you, or thirsty and give you something to drink? When did we see you a stranger and invite you in, or needing clothes and clothe you? When did we see you sick or in prison and go to visit you?' The King will reply, 'I tell you the truth, whatever you did for one of the least of these brothers of mine, you did for me'" (Matt. 25:37-40).

O—— *Our attitude will soon be apparent to those we serve.* In I Thessalonians 5, Paul encouraged the believers to "Hold [those who serve in the church] in the highest regard in love because of their work" (vs. 13). How will your volunteers experience this attitude of high regard? You will be there for them—solving conflicts, prodding the lazy, encouraging the timid, responding with patience and kindness, spreading a spirit of joy, praying for their needs, giving thanks even in trying circumstances (see vss. 14-18). What a gift to those we serve!

Help Your Volunteers Be Successful

Jesus said His leaders were to excel in servanthood. *What is a servant? Someone who helps make others successful.* As Sunday school superintendent or director of children's ministries or children's pastor, you have a wonderful opportunity to help make your volunteers successful teachers. Don't be satisfied with simply filling all your volunteer slots; desire to see your volunteers grow in ministry.

Get excited about making them successful! Catch a vision for what each volunteer will become as Christ works in and through them to reach children. There are several key things you can do to help your volunteers be fulfilled and satisfied with the job they are doing:

O—— *Discern what age level they would be best teaching.* A volunteer who's struggling with junior highs may be top-notch with primaries.

O—— *Be sensitive to their needs.* Don't wait for volunteers to come to you. Initiate asking what they need to do their job. Do they have adequate equipment and supplies? Do they need a

Godly leadership is not power
and "lording it over" others
but loving, humble service.

helper? Is the class too large? Notice their level of enthusiasm within the classroom. When you sense that all is not well, telephone them or talk in person to discover their frustrations.

Support their weak areas; build on their strengths. Serving your teachers means helping the weaker ones experience success, too. The apostle Paul said, "Warn those who are lazy; comfort those who are frightened; take tender care of those who are weak; and be patient with everyone" (I Thess. 5:14, TLB). Work with them to help them be achievers. Help them find their best system of teaching and organization.

It's so rewarding to see the reticent volunteer—the one that said to you, "Kids aren't really my bag, but I know you need the help"—become confident and comfortable with children. It's an even bigger thrill when the children say to them, "Thanks for being my teacher!" This is what it's all about—helping our volunteers become successful!

As you meditate on the Scriptures above, ask God to give you a servant's heart and the "highest regard in love" for each member of your staff. Then, in the space below, list the names of your most recent volunteers and write one or two admirable qualities that you see in each one.

Turning the key:

List some of the practical ways you will demonstrate a servant attitude with your volunteers: ______________________________

____

____

____

____

SUPPORT 2

PROVIDE

solid training

"I can hardly wait to hear her tips on keeping eighth graders in line!"

When you have mastered this key, you will be able to:

- *Choose topics for teacher orientation.*
- *Create expectations for regular attendance.*
- *Organize a way for volunteers to order supplies.*

How to Give Your Volunteers The Training They Need

The most essential support your volunteers need is solid training. Teachers feel insecure and frustrated when they are ill-equipped for the job they are given to do. You can strengthen them by equipping them for their task—before they begin *and* along the way.

Orientation

Before classes begin, introduce volunteers to the organization of the program and basic preparation for teaching. During orientation you might:

1. Present the purpose of Christian education.
2. Discuss your program goals.
3. Familiarize volunteers with student text, teacher's guide, and resources.
4. Teach good lesson planning.
5. Present available teacher resource materials.
6. Explain how to order supplies and be reimbursed for expenses.
7. Explain procedure for obtaining curriculum each quarter.
8. Describe age-group characteristics of children.
9. Pass out class lists with names, addresses, phone numbers, and other helpful information.
10. Provide names, addresses, phone numbers of teachers, superintendent, and resource persons.

Schedule a significant block of time for orientation, such as a Saturday morning. Include presentations that involve all the teachers, then break into "departments" for going over the curriculum and discussing age-level characteristics of children. A simple lunch together after orientation is a way to welcome and put new teachers at ease.

Orientation could also take the form of a class held once a week for four to six weeks. With this format, you might add sessions on guided conversation, discipline, leading a child to Christ, etc. It would be ideal if all volunteers could complete this class prior to teaching.

In-Service Training

Once volunteers face the challenge of teaching Sunday after Sunday, it's easy to become discouraged and decide nothing significant is happening with their class. In-service training can help develop skills and build on experience, providing much-needed support. Here are some keys to make it happen:

Make it an expectation. In your initial interview with volunteers, tell them part of the requirement for ministering to children is to attend regular teacher training. Veteran teachers probably don't think they need any training. But one of the key reasons for holding regular teacher training is to

Teachers feel insecure when they are ill-equipped for the job they are given to do.

build team spirit, develop vision for ministry, and learn from one another.

O—* *Make it regular*. If possible, hold this training once a month; otherwise, once a quarter. Always hold the meeting on the same day of the month—for example, the fourth Tuesday. Then there won't be any excuse for not knowing when the meeting is set. But . . .

O—* *Always send out a notice* a few days prior to the meeting just as a courtesy. (See Resource II-2A for sample postcards.) Or make your own flyer with more information. Besides giving the time and place, state what will be happening at the meeting. Make the notice attractive, using colored paper, fun clip art (Resource II-2B), and warmness in the tone—but also let them know you expect to see them there.

O—* *Do it with excellence!* People are busy today. Respect your volunteers by making the training worthy of giving up an evening for. Depending on the needs of your volunteers, some meetings should be all together; others can be by departments for all or part of the time. Include hands-on training for Bible-learning activities, finger play and song lessons, teaching techniques, maintaining positive discipline, as well as some inspirational meetings.

Many publishers have teacher training idea kits and manuals available. Whatever curriculum you are using, you should be able to adapt the teacher training materials to your own needs.

O—* *Give out prizes* to the classes that have perfect attendance at the meetings. Make the prizes fun and useful—such as a fancy bar of soap, ice cream gift certificates, etc. As volunteers arrive, have each one sign in. Those that miss the meeting should receive a cute postcard (see Resource II-2A) mailed the day after the meeting saying you missed them and were aware of their absence.

Classroom Observation

Along with on-going training, regularly observe in the classroom to see what is happening. This may give you ideas for areas that need to be addressed in your training times. You may also sense some discouragement that you could address one-on-one. You only need to do this twice a year, unless you see a potential problem arising.

Outside Conferences

Encourage your entire teaching staff to attend yearly conferences once in a while. If possible, take the church bus or car pool, and above all, attend with them. Hearing new ideas will be both reassuring and stimulating.

Along with on-going training, regularly observe in the classroom to see what is happening.

Curriculum/Supplemental Materials

Provide teachers with a written curriculum. Not only is teaching a much easier job when a curriculum is available, it also gives you control over what is being taught in the classroom. It isn't wise to let each volunteer do whatever is right in his or her own eyes. A planned curriculum provides scope and sequence to the overall teaching of your children's ministry. You will be assured that all children will cover the entire Bible over a certain number of years.

Budget a supplies fund. Volunteers can do a much better job if they do not have to purchase their own supplies for crafts and holidays. Keep them supplied! Obtain a lockable closet or cupboard for children's ministry supplies.

Organize a system for volunteers to order and receive supplies. (A volunteer supply coordinator will also be a timesaver for you.) For instance:

1. Provide teachers with order forms for supplies (Resource II-2C).
2. Train teachers to order supplies ahead of time.
3. Pass completed order forms to supply coordinator.
4. The supply coordinator fills the orders from the supply closet, then purchases extra things requested that are not kept on hand.
5. The supply coordinator places the order in the classroom. The next Sunday when the teachers arrive, the supplies are waiting.

This method saves you and your volunteers much frustration trying to obtain supplies at the last minute. Give out the telephone number of the supply coordinator so that teachers may call that person with questions and requests.

Turning the key: Plan your first meeting!

Date: __________ Theme: ______________________________

Leader: ______________ Refreshment: __________________

Other ideas: ____

SUPPORT 3

PRACTICE

regular communication

"Our Sunday school superintendent sure has gotten creative since the photocopier broke."

When you have mastered this key, you will be able to:

- *Communicate information to your staff.*
- *Receive feedback from your staff.*
- *Keep in touch personally with individuals.*

How to Set Up A Communication Network

The volunteer feels valued when there is regular and consistent communication among children's ministry staff. But the communication flow must go both ways. Volunteers need regular information to keep them in touch with things they need to know *and* some means of communicating their ideas, problems, and questions through appropriate channels for action.

Write a Regular Newsletter

A weekly or monthly newsletter that could be hand delivered on Sunday mornings or Wednesday evenings is a perfect way to convey important information to the whole staff. Different sections might include:

- pertinent information or news
- prayer requests
- announcements
- last week's attendance
- dates of upcoming events
- a highlight of one of your teachers or helpers
- a craft idea, finger play, or teaching technique
- an article from your heart.

Resource II-3A provides the type and graphics for a sample newsletter that you can easily create. Photocopy the resource sheet and cut out the various components. Then type the date and your various news items on clean sheets of paper, leaving appropriate blank spaces for the nameplate, headings, etc. With rubber cement affix the relevant type and graphic components such as the nameplate and the heading titles you wish to use. When appropriate, add pieces of clip art from Resource II-2B or that you obtain from other sources. Use these masters as you photocopy your newsletter on two sides creating enough copies for your whole staff.

Newsletters help keep all *volunteers informed.* On Monday the newsletter could be mailed to teachers who were absent on Sunday.

If you have time, jot a note across the top of the newsletter that says, "Missed you yesterday" or "Hope you had a good weekend away." The personal touch lets them know you really did miss them.

Visit Every Classroom Personally

It will be an encouragement to your volunteers to see you in their room frequently. As much as possible visit all your Sunday school, children's church, or midweek programs every time they meet. I make it a practice just to walk through the room and smile at or give a word of encouragement to every volunteer if they are not involved in dialogue with a child. I drop off my newsletters

Each week I walk through the classrooms and smile at or give a word of encouragement to every volunteer.

at the same time I am making rounds to every department. Your volunteers need the reassurance that someone knows they are in the trenches every week when the children come romping into the classroom or club meeting.

Communicate with your presence. Make it a practice not to substitute in classes on Sundays or midweek. Getting tied down in a substitution task makes you unavailable to circulate among the other classes to answer questions, help with emergencies, get last-minute supplies, and generally oversee the whole children's ministry.

Make Personal Telephone Calls

Regular telephone calls are a must! It is simply too hectic on Sunday mornings or during your midweek program to try to have any valuable communication one-on-one with your volunteers. Try to telephone each teacher at least once a quarter (once a month, if possible) to see if there are problem areas they need help with, or just to see how they are doing personally.

Ask questions such as: What is your greatest frustration? What is your greatest joy? How can I or other staff be helpful to you? What can I pray about for you? Also, be sure volunteers have your telephone number or the number of their department head so they can call with a question or need.

Depending on the size of your children's ministry, telephoning may need to be delegated to each department coordinator. But phone calls are a valuable way to build rapport and to let volunteers know you are interested in them as co-laborers in Christ.

Ask for Feedback

No news is not necessarily good news when dealing with volunteers in children's ministry. Many are quietly frustrated and become ineffective or suddenly quit.

Don't wait for them to come to you. Build times for feedback into your communication network. During staff meetings, phone calls, or even teacher training events, ask questions similar to the above. Add others appropriate to the age group: What is the best thing about our department? How can it be improved? How do parents react to our Bible teaching program? Where do you feel the need for better communication? In what areas do you desire additional training?

Personal feedback is important. But you may also want to use a written evaluation at mid-year, at the end of the year—or both. See Resource II-3B for a possible evaluation tool.

No news is not necessarily good news
when dealing with volunteers
in children's ministry.

Communication is such a vital part of supporting your volunteers! Don't neglect this important aspect of ministering to them. Choose one of the support keys to begin a regular network of communication.

Turning the key: Jot down three ways you will better communicate with your volunteers.

1. ____

____

____

2. ____

____

____

3. ____

____

____

SUPPORT 4

GIVE

generous doses of appreciation

"No, it's not my birthday—but I do lead children's church."

When you have mastered this key, you will be able to:

- *Choose from several appreciation events.*
- *Find ways to personally affirm volunteers.*
- *Get to know volunteers more intimately.*

How to Show Appreciation to Your Volunteers

All of us need the support and reinforcement that comes when people express their appreciation. How can we affirm all the sacrifices our volunteers make in order to minister to the children in our midst?

Organize Appreciation Events

Consider one or more of these key events to show church-wide support throughout the year for volunteers in children's ministry.

Schedule an "Appreciation Sunday." Plan a variety of special things to happen on the appointed day. For instance:

- Put up a poster board on the door of each classroom for parents to write notes of praise and thanks to their children's teachers.
- Treat teachers to coffee and muffins that morning. Invite them to arrive early, or serve it in a central location so volunteers may drop in at their convenience.
- Parents are usually more than happy to give a small donation to purchase corsages and boutonniere for the volunteers to wear on that day.
- In the morning worship, ask the pastor to recognize teachers with a prayer of thanksgiving and continued blessing on their ministry. This is most effective if volunteers come to the front where all can see them.

Plan an "Appreciation Dessert." Make this a special evening with cloth tablecloths and china dishes. (Stay away from paper if you can. Somehow the "real thing" says this is a special occasion.) A "party favor" on each plate, such as a silk flower with a ribbon or a small box of chocolates, adds a nice touch. And above all, don't ask your volunteers to bring the dessert! If you can't afford it out of the budget, solicit one of the adult Sunday school classes, some of the seniors, or the parents of the children to prepare the dessert for your volunteers. (It's nice if all prepare the same recipe.) Ask a group in the church—perhaps some of the high school students, the senior citizens, or parents—to serve them that evening. Invite a special speaker to speak words of encouragement and/or have someone give a testimony regarding how a particular Sunday school teacher or club leader greatly impacted his or her life as a child. Include some special music in the program. Arranging for some of the children to sing is always a treat and gives the children an opportunity to say, "Thank you," as well. A slide presentation of the various classes, using songs of thanks as background music, would also show teachers how special they are.

"A cheerful look
brings joy to the heart."

Host a "Christmas Open House." Christmas is always a good time to open your home for volunteers to drop by and enjoy a casual evening of fellowship with others involved in your church's children's ministry. It can be simple fare as far as food is concerned. Cookies and punch/coffee/tea would be adequate.

If you can manage it, make or purchase a Christmas ornament for each one to take home. Use your creativity! It is a treat for the volunteers to be in your home and helps create friendship bonds. In the rush of Sunday morning classes and training times, there is usually no time to just visit or hear about their personal interests. An open house is a warm way of saying, "Be my friend, come on over to my house."

End (or begin) the year with a "Children's Ministry Barbecue"—for teachers, children, and their parents. At our church we have family games, a sing-along time, a personal testimony from someone that has gained through the influence of a godly adult, and sharing regarding the significance of the work volunteers are involved in. The presence of the senior pastor or other members of the pastoral staff helps convey the message that the service of volunteers is an important part of the church's ministry.

Give a "Children's Ministry T-Shirt." A highlight of the barbecue (or any of the other appreciation events) could be awarding to each volunteer a T-shirt with the children's ministry logo or theme verse on it. As these T-shirts are worn around the church campus, interest will be generated toward the children's ministry. These T-shirts can be made with clip art, or a drawing someone in the congregation or even one of the children has done. (See Resource II-4A for suggestions.)

Give Personal Appreciation

Verbal affirmation can never be overdone. Look for ways to give volunteers lots of personal praise and encouragement. Proverbs 15:30 tells us, "A cheerful look brings joy to the heart, and good news gives health to the bones." Here are some key suggestions to bring joy to the heart:

Send appreciation notes. Try to write a note of appreciation twice per year to each volunteer. Send at least one card for no particular reason other than to say thank you for his or her faithful service. It's especially encouraging if you can write something personal on the note, even if you just comment on the way she always arrives early or the way you observed him helping a child on a particular day or even her cheerful

"I was so tired and discouraged,
I just wanted to quit.
Then your note came . . ."

smile. Many times I have had a volunteer say, "I was so tired and discouraged, I just wanted to quit. Then your note came this week in the mail and it reassured me that someone does know that I am ministering every week. Thank you for remembering me."

Why not send a note (Resources II-4B through II-4D) to someone today!

Send birthday cards to each volunteer. Keep a card file of the birth dates of your volunteers by the month so that you can send each of them a birthday card. Include a note of thanks and appreciation for the ministry they are involved in; make it as personal as you can. You might write these cards once each month at one sitting, then mail them the week of the birthday.

Now choose one event from the list above and begin your plans. Also, list other ways you can show appreciation to your volunteers.

Turning the key: My plans for an appreciation event . . .

Event: ______________________________

Date: ______________________________

Time: ______________________________

Other ways I can show appreciation to my volunteers. . . ______________________________

____

____

____

SUPPORT 5

PRAY

regularly for your volunteers

"Sorry, I won't be able to go on the free Caribbean cruise—I have an appointment to pray for my volunteers that week."

When you have mastered this key, you will be able to:

- *Cover your children's ministry in prayer.*
- *Support specific prayer needs of volunteers.*
- *Develop prayer support among volunteers.*

How to Support Volunteers Through Prayer

For those involved in leading children's ministries, it's difficult to spend time in prayer. But you are too busy *not* to pray! Prayer helps bring about the results which will benefit your ministry the most. Every person must find his or her own method and time schedule to pray. But you must pray sometime! Be in regular communication with the Lord regarding the needs of your ministry. He is ever present, whether you are recruiting volunteers or supporting them in the classroom.

Pray for Your Children's Ministry Needs

"The harvest is plentiful but the workers are few. Ask the Lord of the harvest, therefore, to send out workers into his harvest field" (Matt. 9:37). God's guiding hand will lead you to willing volunteers as you talk with Him each day. But remember, pray specifically. Ask God for each need. "Today I need a sixth-grade teacher"; "Please send someone to help with bulletin boards"; and so forth.

Pray for Your Volunteers

Once a new volunteer has stepped forward, it becomes your obligation to support him or her in prayer. I pray systematically through each age level as I walk in the morning, praying for each volunteer by name. This places a burden on me to become acquainted with each one. I need to know what their needs are if I am to pray in a specific way. Knowing the dynamics of each classroom also gives me direction to pray for individual problems or children.

Some other key suggestions:

Make a picture prayer album. Take a picture of each teacher, helper, club leader, or choir leader that ministers to children. File them in an album by classroom or club, and then use the prayer album during your prayer time. The faces of the ones you don't know so well will become familiar to you, and help you bond with them.

Find a prayer partner. Enlisting a prayer partner will be a great encouragement to you. Nothing increases our faith faster than witnessing answers to prayer. Ask God for the right person to help you pray for the needs of children's ministry. There may be someone in your church that God has prepared just for you, one that has a deep burden for children. If possible, meet to pray once a week or so depending on your mutual availability. Touch base by telephone whenever necessary to share requests. And by all means always call to share answers to prayer.

Knowing the dynamics of each classroom gives me direction to pray for individual problems or children.

Highlight a volunteer. If you publish a children's ministry newsletter, include a highlight of one of the volunteers each time. Give pertinent information regarding family life, hobbies, length of service, how long attending the church, etc. Design this "Teacher Highlight" to be torn off, so that others can place it on the refrigerator or in their Bibles as a reminder to pray for the volunteer during the coming weeks.

Involve Volunteers in Prayer

Develop prayer partners for volunteers. Prayer partners among the volunteers is a great way to involve them in the total ministry of the Sunday school, children's church, or midweek program. At your regular teacher training meeting, ask everyone to draw names for prayer partners. They will be responsible to pray for their partners for three months (or other predetermined time). At the beginning of every meeting allow time for prayer partners to meet for five to ten minutes to share answers to prayer and current needs for their departments. Every three months redraw names, praying for the needs of the new partners. Volunteers will feel part of each other's ministry through the medium of prayer. It also gives them the responsibility of helping you lift the ministry before the Lord through prayer.

Advertise prayer requests. Make use of your newsletter to make appropriate prayer requests known to all the volunteers.

Encourage prayer for specific children. Involving volunteers in prayer sets an example of the need for prayer as they minister to children. Prayer needs may include problem children, the ones who cause chaos in the classroom. Urge them to pray for the shy child, who also has special needs. Each volunteer will have particular classroom needs, including times of crisis which may involve sick children or death in the family. But it is a real encouragement to the rest of the group to see the answers God will send!

Pray for the shy child
who also has special needs.

Turning the key: Ministry needs I can pray about . . .

Names of volunteers and their specific needs to pray for . . .

RESOURCES

Sample Logos For Children's Ministry

CLASS PROFILE

Class: ____

Room location: ____________________ Approx. sq. ft. ________

Day/Time:____

Average attendance: ________________________________

____ adults per _____ children

Class secretary: ________________________ Phone: ___________

Department leader: ______________________ Phone: ___________

Teacher: ______________________________ Phone: ___________

Teacher/helper: ________________________ Phone: ___________

Teacher/helper: ________________________ Phone: ___________

Teacher/helper: ________________________ Phone: ___________

Future personnel needs: ____________________________

____

____

____

____

____

NEEDS AT A GLANCE

Nursery No. of Children: ___ Supervisor: ___ Helpers: ___	**Nursery** No. of Children: ___ Supervisor: ___ Helpers: ___	**First Grade** No. of Children: ___ Teacher: ___ Volunteers: ___	**First Grade** No. of Children: ___ Teacher: ___ Volunteers: ___
Twos No. of Children: ___ Teacher: ___ Volunteers: ___	**Twos** No. of Children: ___ Teacher: ___ Volunteers: ___	**Second Grade** No. of Children: ___ Teacher: ___ Volunteers: ___	**Second Grade** No. of Children: ___ Teacher: ___ Volunteers: ___
Threes No. of Children: ___ Teacher: ___ Volunteers: ___	**Threes** No. of Children: ___ Teacher: ___ Volunteers: ___	**Third Grade** No. of Children: ___ Teacher: ___ Volunteers: ___	**Third Grade** No. of Children: ___ Teacher: ___ Volunteers: ___
Fours No. of Children: ___ Teacher: ___ Volunteers: ___	**Fours** No. of Children: ___ Teacher: ___ Volunteers: ___	**Fourth Grade** No. of Children: ___ Teacher: ___ Volunteers: ___	**Fourth Grade** No. of Children: ___ Teacher: ___ Volunteers: ___
Fives No. of Children: ___ Teacher: ___ Volunteers: ___	**Fives** No. of Children: ___ Teacher: ___ Volunteers: ___	**Fifth Grade** No. of Children: ___ Teacher: ___ Volunteers: ___	**Fifth Grade** No. of Children: ___ Teacher: ___ Volunteers: ___
Substitutes Class: Teacher/Volunteer:	**Substitutes** Class: Teacher/Volunteer:	**Sixth Grade** No. of Children: ___ Teacher: ___ Volunteers: ___	**Sixth Grade** No. of Children: ___ Teacher: ___ Volunteers: ___

Resource I-2B,

PRAYER LOG

	Personnel Needed	God Answered With . . .	Date Person Began Teaching
1.			
2.			
3.			
4.			
5.			
6.			
7.			
8.			
9.			
10.			
11.			
12.			
13.			
14.			
15.			
16.			

Dream Sheet

Fill out the following statements as though there were no limitations on money, space, time, or personnel. Think: "What would God like to see happen?"

Things I'd like to be doing with my class . . .

To do this, the class would need the following teachers/helpers . . .

The ideal teacher/student ratio for my class would be . . .

Specific areas of interests/skills/resources I'd like to see in future volunteers . . .

Parent-of-the-Week Program

To all classrooms:

As soon as possible we would like to put into effect a program we will be calling, "Parent of the Week" (or "Parent of the Month"). This program will be set up in our preschool through third grade classes. Here's how it works:

1. Each week in your classroom, you will place the children's names (regular attenders) in a container. Explain to the children that someone's parent(s) will be visiting your class each week (month) as a special guest. Then draw a name from the container, announce the name, and tell the child that his or her mom and/or dad will be invited to be "Parent(s) of the Week" next class.

2. Fill out one of our pre-printed invitations (Resource I-5B) and hand it to that child's parent(s) when they come to pick up their child. If this isn't possible, mail the invitation on Monday.

3. During the next week, preferably closer to the end of the week, you need to telephone the parent(s) and ask them if they will be able to come to the class. If you're calling a two-parent home, encourage one or both to attend. If you are calling a single-parent home, make sure this parent feels just as welcome to participate. If no one is able to come, select another parent or set of parents in your room and telephone them.

4. You will need to keep records so you do not repeat parents until all other parents have participated, or been invited to participate. You will want to give all parents the opportunity to be there.

5. When the parent or parents come to your class, have a special place for them to sit and introduce them at the appropriate time, or have their child introduce them. They might also want to say a few words about themselves. The basic reason for their visit is to observe what is happening in your class. Make them aware that they are special guests for that day. They should be encouraged to visit with the other children in the class or help with easy projects (if they expressed a desire to do so). Be sure to tell them they are welcome to visit your classroom anytime.

6. This program will take your personal attention to be successful. You will need to take the time to follow up, perhaps call the parents the next week and tell them how glad you were that they came to their child's class.

7. It's quite possible that some parents may volunteer to come back to the class as helpers at some later date. If so, great! Give them some specific area of responsibility (e.g., crafts, snacks, work with the boys, etc.) that they would enjoy doing.

We want parents to know what is happening in our children's ministry. This program gives them a chance to find out without having to make a substantial commitment of time. It will also serve as an introduction for those who may want to work in children's ministry at some point in the future.

Thank you for your help in making this program a success.

The "Parent of the Week"

in our classroom

on Sunday.

We would be honored

if you would join us

in Room_____ at_____.

Sincerely,

Resource I-5B

Children's Ministries Are For

Adventure (each child is unique)

Discovery (of new and old truths)

Understanding (their needs)

Love (to be given and received)

Teaching (open hearts and minds)

Serving (as Jesus did)

Do you feel inadequate? *We'll train you!*
Don't know where to start? *We'll help you!*
Don't think you have time? *Make your time more significant!*

(Please fill out and turn in to an usher or the information booth.)

Name: ______________________

Phone: ______________________

Age-groups of interest: ______________________

Let the Children

Come to Jesus . . .

. . . with YOU leading the way.

Our goal in ministering to children is to make each child feel loved and valued. In order for us to do this we need many committed and caring people. Won't you consider serving the children at this time in the context of our church's children's ministry?

(Please fill out and turn in to an usher or the information booth.)

Name: ______________________

Phone: ______________________

Age-groups of interest: ______________________

Bear Fruit... Fruit That Will Last

Are you aware that 85 percent of all born-again conversions occur between the ages of 4 and 14? We have a harvest field before us! Won't you join us in reaching our children with the Good News? Our Sunday school needs volunteers now.

(Please fill out and turn in to an usher or the information booth.)

Name: ______________________________

Phone: ______________________________

Age-groups of interest: ______________________________

Want to Perk Up Your Summer?

YOU could perk up your summer by having a ministry with the children of our church. Each summer we are in need of teachers and helpers to fill in on Sunday mornings and in midweek programs for those who are on vacation. The children will love it . . . and so will you!

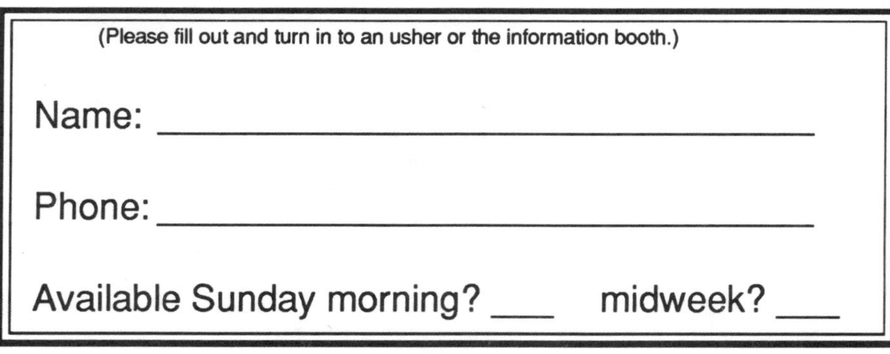
(Please fill out and turn in to an usher or the information booth.)

Name: ______________________________

Phone: ______________________________

Available Sunday morning? ___ midweek? ___

Photocopy the ribbons or buttons of your choice onto heavy, colored paper. Or create a design that suits your church's children's ministry. Cover the photocopied sheets front and back with clear, adhesive plastic (shelf paper).Then cut out the buttons and ribbons and provide pins for your volunteers to attach them so they can be worn on Sunday.

Welcome!

Dear Friend,

Thank you for expressing an interest in becoming a part of the children's ministry in our church. We strive to carry out all children's programs with excellence.

Our goal for all children attending our program is that each one will feel loved and valued as an individual person. We seek to teach Scripture in such a way that it will become evident in their lives at home, at school, and at play. We want to build positive relationships between children and the adults that represent Christ to them.

Since the role of the adult is so vitally important to the children, we ask you to complete the following information sheet and prayerfully consider the responsibility of such a commitment. It will be, for you, a time of hard work, personal sacrifice, and wonderful growth as you labor with the Lord for the salvation and nurturing of His children.

In His service,

PERSONAL INFORMATION SHEET

Name: ______________________________ Phone: __________

Address: ____

Employment: _________________________ Phone: __________

Is it okay to telephone you at work? ________

Single ❏ If married, spouse's name: ____________________

Children's names/ages: _________________________________

____

Birthday (day/month): _________________________________

Hobbies/Interests: ___________________________________

Are you a Christian? _____ On the back of this form, please describe your spiritual journey.

What is your length/level of involvement in this church?
- ❏ Member? How long? _________
- ❏ Nonmember How long attending? _________
- Sunday worship (regularly) ❏ (occasionally) ❏
- Sunday school (attend) ❏ (teach/help) ❏
- Other participation: ______________________________
- Other service: __________________________________

Previous experience in children's ministry (describe).____________

____

I am particularly interested in working with . . .

❏ infants/toddlers	❏ 4th–6th grade
❏ preschool	❏ mid-week program
❏ 1st–3rd grade	❏ children's choir

Teacher Job Description

Your responsibilities include:

A. Personal:

1. Must be a born-again believer in Jesus Christ, who exhibits a consistent testimony and godly walk.
2. Complete the "Personal Information Sheet" and the "My Covenant" sheet concerning service in the children's ministry.
3. Attend worship services regularly.
4. Spend regular time in the Word of God.

B. Assist your department by . . .

1. Preparing all assigned activities *before* Sunday morning.
2. Carrying out specific assigned activities.
3. Guiding children from one activity to another and maintaining an effective learning and worship environment.
4. Cultivating friendships with your co-workers.
5. Praying for the co-workers in your department.

C. Show personal concern to students by . . .

1. Praying for them regularly.
2. Showing a personal interest in your students and their families.
3. Arriving on time—twenty minutes before class begins!
4. Having a neat personal appearance. (Fresh breath is important.)
5. Getting a good night's rest, so you are at your peak of pleasantness.

D. Show personal concern for the church by . . .

1. Returning all equipment and supplies to appointed areas.
2. Modeling to students respect for rooms and furniture.

E. Time involvement:

1. Length of term is normally one year.
2. Three to six hours weekly, including outside preparation.
3. Give adequate notice on Sundays when you'll be absent and find a replacement for yourself from among approved substitutes.
4. Attend *all* scheduled teacher training meetings.
5. Take advantage of outside training opportunities.

My Covenant

Name: ____

Position desired: ________________________________

Age group/grade level: ___________________________

Day: __________________ Hour: ________________

Room: ____

I have prayerfully considered working in the children's ministry in the above position. Realizing the importance to the children to maintain continuity and security in their lives, I am committing myself for a period of ________________, from __________ to __________. At the end of this time I will re-evaluate and pray to determine further commitment.

I agree to be present each week with the exception of illness, vacations, and occasional out-of-town weekends. If I cannot be present, I agree to contact ________________ as soon as I know I will be unable to teach, so a substitute can be obtained.

In addition I will faithfully attend staff meetings and in-service training. If I cannot be present, I will contact

________________________.

Signed: ______________________________________

Date: __________________

Memo to Junior-Helpers

Hello!

We are glad for your interest in the Junior-Helper Program. You have skills and gifts we can use, and we need your help. This experience can also be a learning time for you, not just baby-sitting.

As a Junior-Helper, you should:

- Exhibit appropriate behavior as a role model to younger children.
- Have a genuine interest in younger children.
- Attend Sunday school or worship regularly.

As a Junior-Helper, please remember:

- Have a neat personal appearance.
- Be faithful to be present with your assigned class each week.
- If you'll be absent, let the teacher know at least three days ahead.
- Do not bring any friends to class.

For class time, Junior-Helpers should:

- Read the lesson in the teacher's manual before coming to class.
- Arrive fifteen minutes before class begins.
- Listen to instructions carefully.
- Assist the teacher with the children, crafts, or other activities.

We hope this experience will be enjoyable for you. If you have any questions or problems, please speak to your assigned teacher or to me. We want to assist you in any way we can.

In His service,

Your assigned group is: ________________ Room: _____________

Day: ______________ Time: ___________

Head teacher: _____________________________ Phone: ________

Memo to Children's Ministry Staff
Re: The Junior-Helper Program

Dear __________________,

The Junior-Helper Program makes use of a valuable resource in our congregation—the junior and senior high young people. It is also an opportunity to begin training these youth for future ministry in the church. These Junior-Helpers are our future teachers, leaders, and helpers. Here's what you can do to use Junior-Helpers to their fullest:

1. Welcome Junior-Helpers as part of your team.
2. Provide a teacher's guide. Ask Junior-Helpers to read the story and be familiar with the lesson before the next class.
3. Assign specific tasks to do, so Junior-Helpers feel useful.
4. Give clear instructions. They may not know what to do until they gain some experience.
5. Be patient with mistakes. Assume Junior-Helpers are there because they want to help and learn.
6. Be sure to affirm them when they are doing a good job!
7. Do not allow Junior-Helpers to bring friends to class at any time, even to "help." Kindly tell the friends that they cannot stay, but if they are interested in becoming Junior-Helpers to contact me.
8. Do not allow Junior-Helpers to come into your classroom unless you have previously been informed that they are assigned to you.
9. If Junior-Helpers are absent and have not let you know ahead of time, please call them during the week to find out why. Let them know that you needed and missed them.
10. Remember, you are their role model. They will be looking to you for direction and watching as you exhibit teaching skills.

I hope you enjoy this relationship with your Junior-Helper! If you have any questions or experience any problems, please let me know.

In His service,

Your Junior-Helper is: ______________________ Phone: ___________

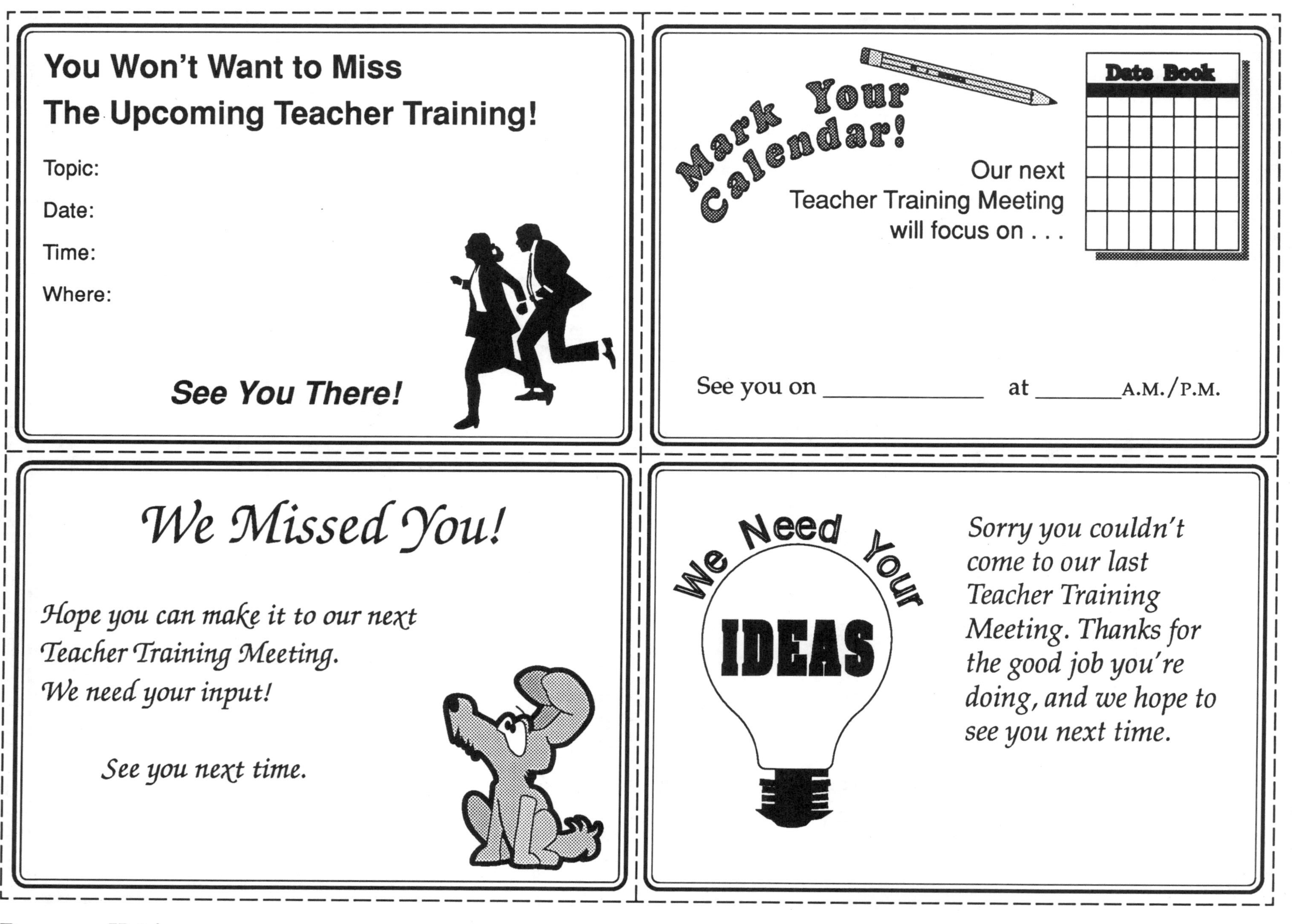

Resource II-2A,

Clip Art Suggestions

Supply Order Form

Person ordering: ______________________________

Class (grade/age level): ______________________________

Room location: ______________________________

Telephone number: ______________________________

Quantity	Item Description (please be specific)
________	______________________________
________	______________________________
________	______________________________
________	______________________________
________	______________________________
________	______________________________
________	______________________________
________	______________________________
________	______________________________
________	______________________________
________	______________________________

(Cut out the nameplate, titles, and symbols on this page to create a newsletter similar to the sample below.)

July 14, 1990

Here's The Scoop On
CHILDREN'S
MINISTRY

LATE NEWS

VOLUNTEERS HONORED

Lorem ipsum dolor sit amet, tus consectetuer adipiscing elit, sed diam nonummy nibh euismod tincidunt ut laoreet dolore magna mik aliquam erat volutpat.

Ut wisienim ad minim veniam, quis nostrud exerci tation ullamcorper suscipit lobortis nisl ut aliquip ex ea commodo consequat.

Duis autem vel eum iriure dolor in hendrerit in vulputate velit esse molestie consequat, vel illum dolore eu feugiat nulla facilisis at vero eros et accumsan et iusto odio dignissim qui

Blandit praesent luptatum ozril delenit augue duis dolore te erat feugait nulla facilisi.

PRAYER REQUESTS

Duis autem vel eum iriure dolor in hendrerit in vulputate velit esse molestie consequat, vel illum dolore eu feugiat nulla facilisis at vero eros et accumsan et iusto odio

Ignissim qui blandit praesent luptatum zzril delenit augue duis dolore te feugait nulla facilisi.

ANNOUNCEMENTS

* Monday, July 16, Nam liber tempor cum soluta nobis eleifend option hendrerit in vulputate.
* Wednesday, July 18, Lorem ipsum dolor sit amet accumsan tifan.
* Friday, July 20, Aliquam erat volutpat om seagun.
* Sunday, July 22, suscipit lobor.

From the Director's Desk . . .

WHY I VISIT EVERY CLASSROOM PERSONALLY

Gobortis velitillum iusto qui. Lorem ipsum dolor sit amet, consectetuer adipiscing elit, sed diam nonummy nibh euismod tincidunt ut laoreet dolore magna aliquam erat volutpat. Ut wisi enim ad minim veniam, quis nostrud exerci tation ullamcorper suscipit lobortis nisl ut aliquip ex ea commodo consequat.

Duis autem vel eum iriure dolor in hendrerit in vulputate velit esse molestie consequat, vel illum dolore eu feugiat nulla facilisis at vero

Craft Idea

Teaching Tip

Puppets

Help Wanted

Assignments

LATE NEWS

PRAYER REQUESTS

ANNOUNCEMENTS

UPCOMING EVENTS

From the Director's Desk . . .

From the Children's Pastor's Desk . . .

TEACHER PROFILE

HELPER PROFILE

WE APPRECIATE . . .

Last Week's Attendance

Thank You, Lord!

LET'S EVALUATE!

Self Evaluation[1]

1. What was your most satisfying experience this year?

2. What was your most disappointing experience this year?

3. As a children's ministry volunteer, what do you do best?

4. How do you feel about yourself and the job you are now doing?

5. What would you like to learn/change in order to do a better job?

General Evaluation

1. What training events have been most helpful to you?

2. How would you evaluate the curriculum and materials you use?

3. Do you have suggestions for better communication among staff?

4. What kind of support/resources do you need in order to do a better job?

5. Please comment on any other areas that could use improvement . . .

1. Adapted from suggestions by Daniel J. Pierson

T-Shirt Idea

T-shirt shops can be found through the yellow pages of your local phone book. They are able to take art work and lettering similar to this sample, enlarge it, and reproduce it on T-shirts. You can use this design or substitute your own. Be sure to get a cost quote before committing to an order.

Sometimes it's a
jungle out there!

Thank you for
making a difference
in the lives
of our children.

And you do it so well!

Thanks!

Working with Children...

...Someone Has to Do It.

Resource II-4C

Thanks so much
for the part you
play in helping
our children grow!

Resource II-4D